Comparing Two Cities

by Anna Lee

I need to know these words.

bicycles

boats

China

city

fish

Italy

Many people live in a city.
A city has many buildings.

▲ These buildings are in a city.

Many people work in a city.
A city is a busy place.

▲ Many people walk on this street.

Look at this city. This city is in China.

China
Beijing

▲ Beijing is a city in China.

Look at this city. This city is in Italy.

▲ Venice is a city in Italy.

The cities are far apart.

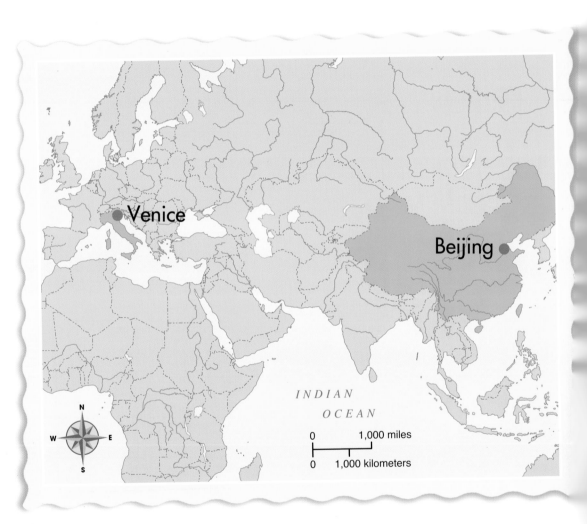

▲ Beijing is far from Venice.

The cities are alike in some ways.
The cities are different, too.

▲ The cities have many people.

You can see many bicycles in this city.

▲ People use bicycles in Beijing.

You can see many boats
in this city.

▲ People use boats in Venice.

Many people in China eat duck.

▲ People in Beijing cook duck to eat.

Many people in Italy eat fish.

▲ People in Venice buy fish to eat.

The weather can be hot in both cities.

Beijing ▶

◀ Venice

▲ The summer can be hot in both cities.

The weather can be cold in both cities.

Venice ▶

▲ Beijing

▲ The winter can be cold in both cities.

People visit both cities. Which city do you want to visit?